IMAGES
of America

PENNSYLVANIA'S COAL
AND IRON POLICE

As if the work was not hard enough, the Coal and Iron Police in many cases made life even harder for coal workers. Pictured here is a miner loading a mining car around 1900. (Luzerne County Historical Society.)

On the cover: Please see page 86. (Daniel J. Burns.)

IMAGES
of America

PENNSYLVANIA'S COAL
AND IRON POLICE

Spencer J. Sadler

ARCADIA
PUBLISHING

Published by Arcadia Publishing
Charleston, South Carolina

Printed in the United States of America

Library of Congress Control Number: 2008939829

For all general information contact Arcadia Publishing at:
Telephone 843-853-2070
Fax 843-853-0044
E-mail sales@arcadiapublishing.com
For customer service and orders:
Toll-Free 1-888-313-2665

Visit us on the Internet at www.arcadiapublishing.com

To all of those who have shown great patience and believed,
and believe me, the list is kind of short.

CONTENTS

ACKNOWLEDGMENTS

Completing the process of writing this book could not have been possible without dragging many people into it. To these people, even those who are unmentioned, who did all they could to play a small part, I say thank you.

Thank you, Stephanie, for being so loving and supportive in all our years together and even more so in the writing of this book. My sons, Morgan and Malcolm, also took interest, and for that I am thankful. Thank you to my parents, Clarence and Marion, who have been extremely supportive of all my endeavors.

The following people, in no particular order, were an immense help by contributing photographs, information, tips, and leads: John Drury, founder and director of the Mauch Chunk Museum and Cultural Center; Ray Washlaski, virtual museum editor, patheoldminer.rootsweb.ancestry.com; Raymond M. Roberts; Amanda C. Fontenova, archivist, Luzerne County Historical Society; Tab Lewis and James Cassedy, National Archives and Records Administration; Harrison Wick, Theresa McDevitt, Rhonda Yeager John Knorr, Laura Krulikowski, and Jean Popovich, the Special Collections Department of Indiana University of Pennsylvania (IUP); Clyde Middleton, Roger Philpot, Lisa Hays (executive director), Ed Hahn, and Joanna Moyar (education coordinator) of the Westmoreland County Historical Society; Robin Lighty and Keith Brady, Department of Environmental Protection (DEP) Bureau of Mining and Reclamation; Alice Yamber, Latrobe Historical Society; Mike Donnelly, president and publisher of the *Indiana Gazette*; James P. Quigel and Lois Fischer, Lehigh University; Pauline and Kathryn Rakosky; Marla Stankus; Randi Marodi; Vicki Molesky; Dave Kuchta; Steve Bachmann, curator, Historical Society of Dauphin County; Ken Lewetag; R. Don Troxel; Charles Greene from Princeton University; Daniel Zyglowicz and Ryan LaQuay, California University of Pennsylvania; William Huber; Jude Wudarczyk, Lawrenceville Historical Society; Marci Bowers and Joe Pittman of Sen. Don White's office; Brenda Galloway, Temple University; Daniel J. Burns; Denise Weber; Tom White, special collections curator and Elizabeth Williams of Duquesne University; Jack Hill; David Haugaard, Historical Society of Pennsylvania; John Busovicki; James T. Parker II, vice president, Double Delta Industries, Inc.; and Bill Hamilton (IUP).

Many thanks also go to Erin Vosgien and Arcadia Publishing for believing that the story of the Coal and Iron Police needs to be told.

Unless otherwise noted, images are from the author's collection.

INTRODUCTION

In 1887, noted historian Lord Acton said, "Power corrupts; absolute power corrupts absolutely." With the absolute power that Pennsylvania's Coal and Iron Police (C&I) possessed with the backing of powerful companies from 1865 to 1931, Acton would say that their moral corruption was inevitable.

Unchecked and untrained, Pennsylvania's company police forces were the manifestation of political pull and elaborate conflicts of interest. With little to no accountability, the end result was the C&I's corruption of morality that was heard and tried in the courts in lawsuits for harassment, physical abuse, rape, and murder. The C&I not only intimately touched individual workers' daily lives, it had a lasting effect on the very towns that it was paid to protect.

The C&I was able to accomplish some good with the power that the governor granted it, but today, the good appears ultimately overshadowed by misdeeds, judicial indifference, and the power to cover up any indiscretions. Innocent civilians suffered great loss, either of loved ones or personal possessions. The abuse of justice was so outrageous and extreme and the stories so salacious that newspapers across the country watched in anticipation of attention-grabbing headlines.

What started as a legitimate form of company and property protection morphed into a controversial form of vigilante law enforcement. Company police could act with little concern for workers' rights because they knew that the miners were little more than indentured servants whose livelihood depended on the company.

Serving as the eyes and ears of the company, officers of the C&I patrolled and reported to their bosses nearly every aspect of the workers' lives. Things like who shopped where, or who was seen conversing with whom, or other details of miners' daily activities were duly noted. The private police protected company property and, even more importantly, the special interests that ensured the companies' profits.

But, like many great kings and rulers throughout history, the C&I officers consumed themselves with hubris, unrelenting lethal prejudice, and unrestrained power, a deadly recipe for failure and extinction.

The industrial police brought about the need for a state-regulated and governmentally funded law enforcement agency. The first of its kind, the Pennsylvania State Police is a direct result of events that took place throughout the age of private police forces in the coalfields.

Other states followed and installed formalized state police forces across the country. However, the Pennsylvania coal companies' political might was so strong that the C&I was able to exist simultaneously with the Pennsylvania State Police for 26 years, despite efforts to eradicate.

The story of Pennsylvania's C&I has never been told comprehensively, chronologically, or objectively. The subject is sporadically breached in the isolated capsules of a specific event, but in widening the scope on the company police, the court battles, and congressional legislation, a strong narrative emerges.

Why was the social experiment of the private police forces swept under the proverbial rug? Although unsavory, the story of the C&I should be held up as a cautionary tale, especially since current events seem to echo particular elements of police brutality and biased justice.

Another key factor is their role as strike-breakers in American history's labor relations. Their immunity to the law, penchant for criminal behavior, and malicious intent was protected by their commission and the organization on the form sent in to the state. If fear, intimidation, or brute force was necessary to deter the miners from assembling and halting production, the C&I seemed to answer the call.

Political and judicial connections gave companies power. In some cases, the prosecutors in the hearings were company officials. In most cases, there were jurors on the company payroll, and, like in the case of the Molly Maguires, the judges were protected day and night by Pinkertons, who were being paid by the coal company.

Today we still have private detectives, security guards, and campus police, some of which are authorized and licensed to carry arms in the tradition of the Pinkertons and the C&I. Yet their power has been limited, their jurisdiction minimized, their regulations tightened, and their activities and backgrounds scrutinized. Although the basic concept is the same, there is essentially no comparison to the C&I forces of the bygone era. Probably because of hard lessons learned.

To visit these small coal-mining towns and to speak with the older generation who either saw firsthand or heard first accounts about the "pussyfoots," Cossacks, gestapo, "yellow dogs," or whatever other name the town had attached to their local company's police force, the stories are threaded together with consistencies, namely respect from fear.

However, some look back today and realize the great challenge that faced the C&I. Living among the workers and following the orders of company administration, they walked a social tightrope. Labor unrest had spurred workers to drastic measures of burning, looting, and threatening or taking the lives of company officials. There were pop shots at the C&I and top brass. Vandalism and destruction of company property was a serious issue that hurt the bottom line. And strikes threatened the welfare of the company and its sheer existence.

In the end, hostile workers were quelled and order ultimately restored by company watchdogs who in some cases killed indiscriminately without recourse or expressed regret. Intimidation tactics kept the workers in check along with the threat of being evicted from their homes. A number of approaches could be used because the C&I could conduct daily business knowing that they were virtually untouchable.

In some extreme cases like in Homestead and Lattimer, tensions elevated to out-and-out warfare that demanded America's attention. But, in most cases, the battles were small-scale and metaphorical, and they took place here and there throughout the coal regions of Pennsylvania on a daily basis. Occasionally, there were casualties of foreign workers, but they always seemed to fail to grab national attention. In fact, at times it seemed that only the families cared.

As in most instances where big business and large sums of money are involved, the C&I became a political matter to be battled out in legislation and the court of public opinion, created by the media, rumor, and speculation.

In 1931, the citizens and political leaders became intolerant of the armed and dangerous private, industrial police and the blatant abuse of power. But, oddly enough, the chord was not pulled in one climatic gesture. Instead, the C&I forces faded gently away one by one as their commissions ran out with the governor refusing to renew or extend them.

The last commission closed a chapter in labor relations history that left a trail of bloodshed and violence in its wake. Is today's mistrust of authority a direct descendant of a virtually autonomous and privatized police system that spawned state agencies? What role did Pennsylvania have in shaping political and social views of labor relations and law enforcement? Are C&I forces responsible for strangling the life out of some Pennsylvania small coal towns and keeping them from growing more prosperous? These questions are central to *Pennsylvania's Coal and Iron Police*.

One

SETTING THE STAGE

To set the stage of Pennsylvania's Coal and Iron Police (C&I), it is important to briefly investigate coal-mining history, the life of the miners, the towns they inhabited, and the mindset of the companies' top brass.

Six days a week, miners endured dark, damp, dangerous, and laborious work in conditions that led to (in one way or another) an untimely death. Immigrants in search of an American dream found themselves in company housing and in essence indentured servitude. Their bosses seemed indifferent to their plight and employed individuals as company police who were known to be vindictive and callous enough to kick the miners and steelworkers while they were down, thus preventing any type of uprising.

The emergence of unionization fueled a revolutionary spirit and gave the miners a boost of morale through the power of numbers. This threatened the well-being of the company, and orders were given to the company police to keep miners from congregating in the streets and to tighten the reins of authority.

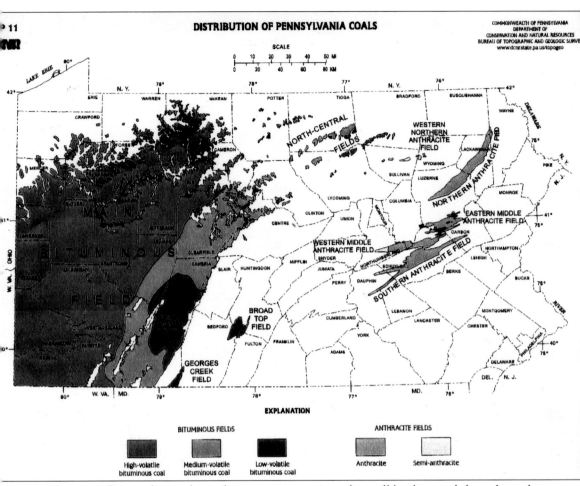

DISTRIBUTION OF PENNSYLVANIA COALS

COMMONWEALTH OF PENNSYLVANIA
DEPARTMENT OF
CONSERVATION AND NATURAL RESOURCES
BUREAU OF TOPOGRAPHIC AND GEOLOGIC SURVEY
www.dcnr.state.pa.us/topogeo

SCALE

EXPLANATION

BITUMINOUS FIELDS

High-volatile bituminous coal

Medium-volatile bituminous coal

Low-volatile bituminous coal

ANTHRACITE FIELDS

Anthracite

Semi-anthracite

This map of Pennsylvania shows the reoccurring regions that will be discussed throughout the book. Bituminous southwestern Pennsylvania and the eastern anthracite fields were heavily populated by a glut of immigrants in search of the American dream. As American homes became more and more dependent on anthracite coal for heating, as the railroad systems grew and demanded more coal for steam engines, and as industrialization and the production of steel required tremendous amounts of bituminous coal in the form coke, Pennsylvania coal "patch" towns sprouted up to answer the demands for anthracite "hard" and bituminous "soft" coal production. Unfortunately, when the companies moved on for fresh mines, the towns for the most part died. Pennsylvania was the nations' largest producer in the early years, and 1918 was the state's historical high. (Don White and the Commonwealth of Pennsylvania Department of Conservation and Natural Resources Bureau of Topographic and Geologic Survey.)

Although undoubtedly coal was known to American Indian hunters and gatherers much earlier, two hunters at two different locations yet somewhat simultaneously are given credit for finding coal in Pennsylvania outcroppings, Nicho Allen and Philip Ginter (Ginder). The documented years vary between 1790 and 1792. Dubbed "the Black Yankee," Allen, a lumberjack, is said to have been camping on a hunting expedition at the foot of Broad Mountain when he built a fire in the evening but awoke in the morning to find that his fire continued burning and growing when it should have been mere embers. Ginter's story is documented with a marker at the site of Sharp Mountain in Summit Hill. His rags-to-riches-to-rags-again story is much more colorful and popular to the people of Pennsylvania since he was eventually exploited and stripped of his land by corporate greed, the blue-collar, us-versus-them motif. (Mauch Chunk Museum and Cultural Center.)

The "ne're-do-well," as he is called
by the Pennsylvania Historical and
Museum Commission, Philip Ginter
showed his accidental find to Col. Jacob
Weiss of the Continental army at
Fort Allen. Weiss and others claimed
10,000 acres of coal-rich territory and
began the Lehigh Coal Mine Company
in 1792. Their attempts to market the
product to Philadelphians was largely
unsuccessful until the land was leased
to Josiah White and Erskine Hazard in
1818. The Lehigh Coal and Navigation
Company (incorporated in 1822), made
up of White, Hazard, and a German
immigrant named George Frederick
August Hauto, had a three-pronged plan
for success. (Left, Historical Society of
Dauphin County; below, Mauch Chunk
Museum and Cultural Center.)

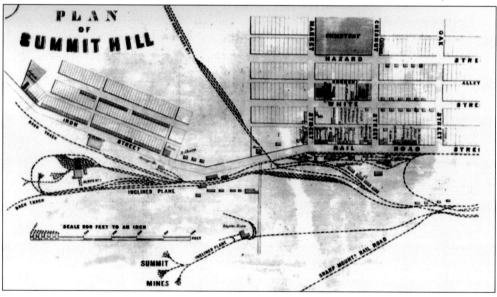

As the Switchback Gravity Railroad Foundation, Inc., outlined, the plan's stated objectives were as follows: "First, they will develop descending river navigation by 1824. Then, they will follow that with ascending navigation by 1838. And, when justified, they will develop a railroad to move coal from Summit Hill to the river landing." The trio got approval to throw the plan into action with the legislators saying, "Gentlemen, you have our permission—to ruin yourselves." The result was one of America's frontrunners of the industrial revolution, and it is also one of the most enduring companies in America that is still in existence today. (Above, Library of Congress; below, Mauch Chunk Museum and Cultural Center.)

Josiah White is grossly overlooked in American history. He accomplished advances in iron and steel manufacturing, bridge construction, coal usage, and the country's first railroad of any significance. Then, importing coal from across the ocean was cheaper than mining and transporting it out of the Pennsylvania wilderness to the market place. White, intent on getting coal to the masses, believed in its potential in home heating. (Library of Congress.)

White sunk his hardware store fortunes into his clever combo of using locks and "bear traps" and a gravity railroad system. Mauch Chunk and Summit Hill Gravity Railroad, also known as the Switch Back, prompted a boom in the coal-mining industry and local tourism, and it offered a model that roller coasters and wild water rapids amusement park rides still use today. (Mauch Chunk Museum and Cultural Center.)

Many of the smaller coal towns sprinkled throughout Pennsylvania's coal regions, known as patch towns, at the dawn of the 20th century did not grow organically. Instead of families congregating in developing municipalities, some Pennsylvania coal towns were established by a company with a sole purpose to use the area's natural resources to mine coal and transport it to the highest bidder. These two pictures of the Clearfield Bituminous Coal Company in Barr Slope (1923) characterize how coal companies efficiently poured their own blocks and constructed towns by building cookie-cutter housing and all the other accoutrements of a self-sufficient, fully functioning society. (IUP Special Collections.)

In an article on her Web site on McIntyre, Susan Ferrandiz quotes a letter written in 1902 by Lucius W. Robinson, an executive of the Rochester and Pittsburgh Coal and Iron Company, to an agent: "We want mainly good Italians, Polanders and Hungarians. We do not want any colored help, or Irish, under any circumstances, nor do we want any hard coal strikers." With a town easily policed on horseback, any outsider or undesirable is easily thwarted. The C&I knew everyone who lived in the town, their personal business, and any regular visitors that they had. As a result, the company's outlook and police presence stifled the town's growth. This 1950 aerial photograph of Ernest typifies the lack of growth that the town, and many like it, has produced in nearly 50 years since the Rochester and Pittsburgh Coal and Iron Company set up shop to mine the area in 1904. (IUP Special Collections.)

In Ernest (named after the grandson of powerful executive Adrian Iselin), the Rochester and Pittsburgh Coal Company purchased the land from farmers and residents and began construction of a town of its own. The company store and the doctor's office (both from 1906) and other necessary infrastructure was provided. The C&I had a strong presence in the little patches of Ernest and Creekside, and more than one resident insinuated that the company police may have consciously turned a blind eye to the crosses being burned and the dynamite blasts in between houses in the name of the Ku Klux Klan. (IUP Special Collections.)

The streets of Commodore were named after Clearfield Bituminous Coal Corporation executives. The town was named after Commodore Cornelius Vanderbilt, founder of Clearfield Bituminous Coal Corporation's subsidiary company the New York Central Railroad. Commodore was a "model" town that offered better accommodations to attract better workers and families. Nothing existed in the area but a couple of farmhouses, a little, local sawmill, and a general store. Between 1919 and 1921, the company built over 100 houses, and even they were impressed with their own expediency. Police presence was virtually nonexistent until 1927, when nonunion miners began organizing. As the photographs illustrate, superintendents' housing is very much different from miners' houses. (IUP Special Collections.)

Mules played a vital part of coal-mining history. Even though they were terribly stubborn and even dangerous (some miners were killed by being kicked in the chest or head, pinned against the mine walls, or pulled under carts), companies placed more value on mules than workers, who could be more easily replaced. During World War I, the *Pottsville Journal* reported that "in some sections of the mining fields, electricity has been substituted for mule power and sooner or later will throw the mule out of his long time job, but many mining companies are not yet in position to use electricity. The scarcity of mules, has accordingly, created a problem that must be met. The shortage has arisen from the demands of the war." (IUP Special Collections.)

The *Pottsville Journal* offered specific numbers in its report: "Just how big of a drop in the market the mule supply has taken can be seen in the United States statistics for the normal conditions preceding the war and the three year period for the fiscal year ending June 30th last. From 1912 to 1914 inclusive the average annual shipment of mules was 4,833. In 1915 there were 65,788 mules sent over the ocean; 111,915 shipped in 1916 and 136,869 in 1917 making a total of 316,572 mules exported since the war for civilization began. . . . It will be seen accordingly, from these figures that the war needs for mules works against the anthracite output, just as the draft and other causes create a loss of 24,000 mine workers from the anthracite region since we entered the war." (DEP Bureau of Mining and Reclamation and the Robin Lighty/Keith Brady Collection.)

Even though oxen, horses, and to a much larger degree mules were part of the mining process well up until the 1950s, in some companies, electric cutters emerged at the dawn of the 20th century. Productivity was drastically increased, and this simple, yet effective machinery paved the way for greater technological and engineering advancements. Dave Kuchta, coal-mining historian, writes, "The commonplace freedoms of labor today—to organize, to bargain, to strike and picket—were claimed at the risk of violence at the hands of employers' goon squads, private armies that had no parallel in other countries. England, France, Canada, and Germany could not compete with America in the bloodiness of labor confrontations. Business was impatient with anything that got in the way of making America richer faster. The middle class resented immigrants and feared 'socialism.' The press reflected and reinforced these emotions. There was no one in the White House to offer a different vision." (IUP Special Collections.)

"Once a man, twice a boy" refers to the life cycle of a miner, up until 1935 when federal labor laws reformed the use of "breaker boys." Young boys and preteens separated slate rock from coal after it had been brought out of the shaft. Teens would often drive the mule teams until adulthood when they would be full-fledged miners. After a long career as a miner, a man would be demoted to children's work once again. (Above, Luzerne County Historical Society; left, Library of Congress.)

In 1920, Joe Joy introduced his model 4BU, the world's first mechanical loader, after honing and pitching the sketches for nearly 17 years since he was 20. The picture above is Dewey Joy, Joe's brother and company sales manager of Joy Machine Company, from a series of promotional photographs from 1915. The first gathering arm loader was shipped to Pittsburgh Coal Company's Sommer No. 2 Mine on September 27, 1916. Joe applied for a patent for this gathering arm loader and continued to work on its testing and development underground, both literally and figuratively. He was awarded a patent, in his name, for the machine in 1919. The photograph below is of the machine in action from 1920. (IUP Special Collections.)

Mechanical mining greatly increased production, but as Eileen Mountjoy Cooper points out from her studies, "Mechanical mining, while it eventually freed the miner from the drudgery of pick and shovel, created many changes in his traditional methods of digging and transporting coal. Instead of two buddies in a room for example, as many as six men sometimes worked together shoveling coal into a 'face conveyor' for removal to the surface. In that case, 'piecework' and payment based on individual tonnage was replaced by daily wages." (Above, IUP Special Collections; left, DEP Bureau of Mining and Reclamation and the Robin Lighty/Keith Brady Collection.)

Whether miners were paid by the hour, day, or ton, wage disputes tore at labor relations and caused strife throughout Pennsylvania coal-mining and steelmaking history. From these disputes, violence and bloodshed erupted. If it was not the harsh, laborious working conditions and unfair wages breaking the spirits of the workers, it was the oppression and intimidation tactics of the ever-present C&I that underscored and accentuated the workers' helplessness and hopelessness. In an attempt to be heard, miners organized themselves, either officially through the union or unofficially by themselves, which was strongly discouraged by the unions. (Duquesne University Archives and Special Collections.)

Workers reportedly walked off their posts without warning or just cause. The United Mine Workers of America (UMWA) discouraged this type of behavior and impromptu walkouts, but that did not keep overworked, sometimes hungover, and bitter laborers from convincing their coworkers to join them in walking away from their jobs for a day or two. Frustrated in voiceless poverty, they attempted to dish out the same as they were being dealt; therefore, they destroyed company property, took pop shots at company policemen, and did what they could to spite the company. In most cases, however, when a miner did not report to work or was believed to be stirring up mischief, the C&I was sent to drag him out of bed or investigate the insubordination. (Duquesne University Archives and Special Collections.)

Another serious concern that dug under the skin of bosses and executives was bootlegging. Usually this consisted of the unemployed, or even the families of the miners, and local residents picking coal that fell from loaded railcars from the banks in broad daylight. Initially it was permitted by most companies, but by 1925, companies' advanced mining efforts were so efficient that lost coal became a thing of the past. Bootleggers' methods of illegal mining also became more advanced and efficient, especially after the C&I disappeared. In effect, the C&I increased efforts to curb this behavior. Dave Kutchta of Coaldale noted that the C&I in his town would cut with a knife bootleggers' burlap sacks if caught on the culm banks. (Above, Luzerne County Historical Society; below, Library of Congress.)

Dave Kuchta wrote about the bootleg miners, which were much more than just children in Scottdale and miners' wives in Hazelton (as pictured) picking coal from the banks. The problem blossomed when the C&I's commissions were pulled. Bootlegging grew so great in the mid-1930s that the governor intervened to stamp out these illegal operations. "Many a family was raised on the money earned at these enterprises. Also, if it was not for the bootleg mine holes, many homes would have been without heat during the winter season. Union miners had a love/hate relationship with 'Bootleggers' . . . The locations of these illegal mine operations were kept secret. Any roads to the operations were kept camouflaged with branches, etc. Most of these mines were slopes driven on a steep pitch." (DEP Bureau of Mining and Reclamation and the Robin Lighty/Keith Brady Collection.)

Daily life for the miners and their families was one of poverty and squalor, yet what little they had was doled out to them by the company. They lived in company housing and shopped on credit at the company store and bought their tools and had them sharpened or maintained by the company (and in many cases had charges taken out of their pay for it). When they needed first aid, they saw the company doctor. And they were "protected" by company police. (Duquesne University Archives and Special Collections.)

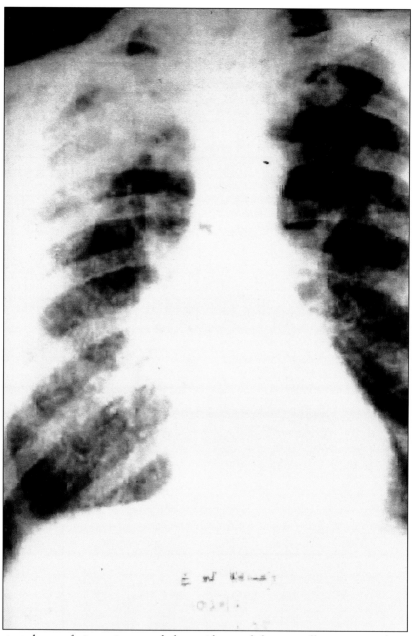

The greatest danger facing miners and the residents of these small towns was the coal dust particles that permeated the air and settled in the lungs and led to pneumoconiosis (CWP) or anthracosis (commonly referred to as black lung), a lung disease with no treatment. Statistics on black lung deaths predating the early 1960s and 1970s are nearly nonexistent, and those that do exist are unreliable. Exposure to coal dust, even in small amounts since the body has no way of ridding the lungs of the deposits or healing the scarring that the coarse particles caused, has long-term effects of shortness of breath and other asthma-like symptoms. Constant exposure means certain death, and residents who did not work in the mines were totally unaware that their lives were in danger because of the black dust that infiltrated the town. (Roger Philpot, www.rogerphilpot.homestead.com.)

Two

THE INCITING INCIDENTS

Against the backdrop of the American Civil War, another revolution was taking place in Pennsylvania railroads and coalfields. Violence ensued, and things were not safe for company executives or their laborers. Two prime examples of the situation at their extremes existed before the dawn of the 20th century. First was the story of the Molly Maguires and their vigilante-style warfare that was an extended battle that left mine bosses and miners dead in its wake. Then there was the Homestead Strike, a situation that some call one of the most important labor disputes in American history. Working in conjunction with company police, both cases highlight a hired army and "the King" of the private police forces, Allan Pinkerton.

Gov. Andrew Gregg Curtin, a steady, guiding hand and conservative "unionist" concerning slavery throughout the Civil War, attempted to quell the violence that plagued Pennsylvania railroad systems by granting the operators the power to employ their own private police forces in 1865 with Act 228. Up until that time, law enforcement primarily consisted of unorganized and untrained county constables and sheriffs, rough-and-tumble, gun-toting ruffians who feared nothing. There was no formal training, background checks, standards, or policies in place to screen or manage these officers who had freedom to interpret the law as they saw fit. The significance of this legislation was not fully realized initially, barely making any kind of impact until years later. Legislation that got more immediate results was his repealing the state tonnage tax, which assisted the Pennsylvania Railroad to become the nation's largest transport system. (Pennsylvania Historical and Museum Commission.)

In 1866, the allowance to employ private police forces was expanded to "embrace all corporations, firms, or individuals, owning, leasing, or being in possession of any colliery, furnace, or rolling mill within this commonwealth." The supplement also mandated that the words, "coal and iron police" appear on the badges, offering some form of differentiation between these industrial police and those sheriffs and constables at the local level and national officials and guardsmen. A total of 7,632 commissions were granted. Mostly only large corporations and profitable companies were able to take advantage of the legislation by establishing their own police force. (Ray Washlaski.)

Allan Pinkerton (left) was born in Glasgow, Scotland, and moved to America at the age of 23. He did not start the first freelance detective agency, but his was undoubtedly the largest and the best. While in Chicago in the late 1840s, his fledgling business had an account with the Rock Island and Illinois Central Railroad. The president of the company was George McClellan, and its attorney was Abraham Lincoln. Years later, Lincoln made Pinkerton head of the first U.S. Secret Service. With professionalism, undaunted ambition, and a successful track record for "getting his man," Pinkerton legitimized and gave credibility to private police forces. He worked on solving and taking part in some of the most notorious cases in American history, and he brought a host of colorful and legendary outlaws to justice. (Historical Society of Dauphin County.)

During the Civil War, Irish terrorists known as the Molly Maguires wreaked havoc and disrupted production in Schuylkill County, then the nation's chief producer. The *Pennsylvania State Archives Miner's Journal of 1867* cites 52 deaths between 1863 and 1867 in that region. Franklin B. Gowen, a Schuylkill county prosecutor, became president of the Philadelphia and Reading Coal and Iron Company. (Historical Society of Dauphin County.)

FRANKLIN B. GOWEN
RULER OF THE READING

In October 1873, Gowen, frustrated with authorities' ineptness, met with Pinkerton in Philadelphia to solicit his involvement. Pinkerton agreed to take the case and assigned James McParland to infiltrate the Mollies and bring them to justice. Posing as James McKenna, a miner from Colorado, McParland became a Molly, collected evidence, and arrested the ringleaders of the gang. (Historical Society of Dauphin County.)

On July 6, 1875, Benjamin Yost, a Civil War veteran and respected officer of the Tamaqua Police, was murdered with a .32-caliber handgun while he was snuffing street lamps for the night. It is assumed that the hit was in retaliation for a previous arrest that he had made. Yost's murder was a turning point as the local citizens formed a committee to attempt to find the killers, turning sympathetic public opinion against the Mollies. Also, James Carroll, a saloon owner where the murder was allegedly planned, was arrested and hanged on June 21, 1877, for the murder of Yost. Unwaveringly claiming his innocence throughout the trial and history, his family erected a monument in Carroll's honor. (Left, Historical Society of Dauphin County; below, Pennsylvania Department of Commerce.)

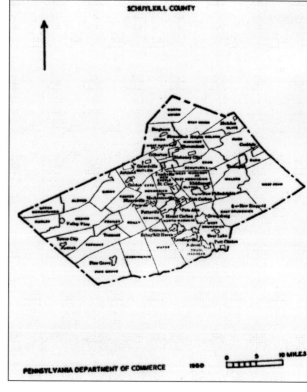

On December 10, 1875, a strange twist in the story of the Mollies took place. At 3:00 a.m., a band of six or seven gunmen burst into Margaret O'Donnell's boardinghouse and murdered Charles O'Donnell and his pregnant sister Ellen McAllister. Charles McAllister, who was Ellen's husband, was wounded during the attack, and he fled for his life. Margaret O'Donnell was pistol whipped. Charles "Black Jack" Kehoe's brother-in-law, a key figure of the Mollies, was suspected of the killing of mine boss Thomas Sanger and miner William Uren. The attack was thought to be pay back. The gunmen of the Wiggans Patch Massacre were never identified or brought to trial, but circumstantial evidence has Allan Pinkerton, Franklin B. Gowen, and James McParland implicated as the masterminds behind the murders. (Historical Society of Dauphin County.)

Incriminating evidence exists today in a letter to Allan Pinkerton penned by James McParland. Soon after the murders, McParland wrote a 44-page letter to Pinkerton asking to be relieved of his duties in Shenandoah. Loretta Murphy documents the entire letter on her Wiggans Patch Web site. He wrote, "Now I wake up this morning to find that I am the murderer of Mrs. McAlister. What had a woman to do with the case—did the [Molly Maguires] in their worst time shoot down women? If I was not here the Vigilante Committee would not know who was guilty and when I find them shooting women in their thirst for blood I hereby tender my resignation to take effect as soon as this message is received. It is not cowardice that makes me resign. . . . I am not going to be an accessory to the murder of women and children." (Library of Congress.)

Pinkerton convinced McParland to continue with his duties, promising that the end of the case was within reach. Pinkerton and McParland, who accepted $12 a week plus paid expenses, followed the case through to its conclusion. McParland's work resulted in 20 suspects being arrested, tried, and executed. Begrudgingly, he testified, and the audience sat in disbelief that the mild-mannered, sophisticated McParland was the same boisterous and drunkenly coarse James McKenna. To the jury, Franklin B. Gowen said, "Is there a man in this audience, looking at me now . . . who longs to point his pistol at me? I tell him that he has as good chance here as he will ever have again. . . . I tell him that if there is another murder in this county by this society, there will be an inquisition for blood with which nothing that has been known in the annals of criminal jurist prudence can compare." Pinkerton's agents offered added security and stood guard at the holding cells for those sentenced to death. (Historical Society of Dauphin County.)

CAPT. R. J. LINDEN

During James McParland's investigation, Allan Pinkerton sent additional detectives to serve as bodyguards without McParland's knowledge. He also sent R. J. Linden, assistant superintendent of the Chicago Pinkerton office, to serve as captain of the C&I with his Pinkerton connections kept secret. In fact, the Flying Squadron, as this regional fraternity of police captains were dubbed, were known to lurk in the shadows of intentional identity obscurity. Linden was also implicated in the orchestration of the Wiggans Patch murders. As longtime war buddies, Pinkerton entrusted Linden to act with autonomy in case of emergency and supported any decision made. Linden's stabilizing force and no-nonsense approach led to an almost immediate decrease in theft, beatings, bar fights, and all-around mischief. By communicating and networking with surrounding counties and mine officials, the effects of his policing were far-reaching. (Historical Society of Dauphin County.)

Although the terror that the Mollies inflicted on Schuylkill, Carbon, Lackawanna, Northumberland, and Columbia Counties is undeniable, some question the very existence of the band. The organization the Ancient Order of Hibernians, of which many Irish Catholic immigrants belonged, was well known and legitimate since its inception in New York in 1835. However, some of today's historians infer that Franklin B. Gowen and Pinkerton sensationalized and manufactured the spin-off terrorist group of the Mollies for nothing more than mere strikebreaking for monetary and political gain. Although this seems cynical, strong arguments make it not that far fetched. (Library of Congress.)

Tainted by speculation, urban legend, and half-truths, the long-term impact on law enforcement because of this incident is unclear. The small town of Mauch Chunk (now Jim Thorpe), whose economy also relied on tourism, never fully recovered from the threat of violence and the one-sided, unjust trial proceedings. (Mauch Chunk Museum and Cultural Center.)

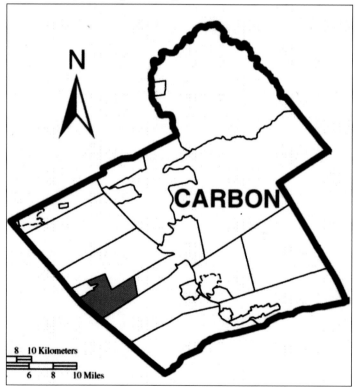

Also, the organization of mine unions was dealt a crushing blow, and, even worse, the public became distrustful of law enforcers and private police forces, knowing of Franklin B. Gowen's manipulation of the justice system and perceiving undercover work as underhanded. (U.S. Census Bureau.)

On the "Day of the Rope," 10 Mollies were hanged. Gov. John Hartranft was criticized for signing death warrants for what many believed to be innocent civilians used as scapegoats. There were biased press coverage and prosecuting attorneys on coal and railroad company payrolls. Most jurors were German and knew little English. Unreliable prosecuting witnesses struck deals for lesser sentences. (Historical Society of Dauphin County.)

Tough on crime and punishment and decorated as a Civil War hero, Hartranft's legacy is besmirched by controversy. Rumor had Hartranft in a pre-reelection pact with "Black Jack" Kehoe, the Molly Maguires ringleader, and a possible pardon for his support that would bring the anthracite regions' vote. Other unsavory later decisions engulf his reputation as governor. (Historical Society of Dauphin County.)

The impact that the Molly Maguires had on unionization can be disputed, but the gross injustices throughout the proceedings cannot be. Judge Cyrus L. Pershing's anti-labor, anti-immigrant biases can be documented in his rulings. Bigotry coupled with the fact that he lost the 1875 governor's election because of Jack Kehoe's borough and other Molly territories raises concern. Some evaluated the "Great Political Conspiracy of 1875" and insinuated that Pershing's sentencing of Kehoe and the Mollies was revenge for a lost election. During the trials, Pershing was protected night and day by Allan Pinkerton's men, paid for by Franklin B. Gowen. In a grim coda, Gowen, who helped pen the legislation for the C&I and lobbied extensively for its passage, was found fatally shot through the head in a Washington, D.C., hotel room on December 13, 1889. R. J. Linden investigated the case and ruled it a suicide. Author Patrick Campbell suspected murder, and with enough raised doubt reopened the case in his convincing 2002 book, *Who Killed Franklin Gowen?* (Historical Society of Dauphin County.)

The Great Railroad Strike of 1877 started on July 14 in Martinsburg, West Virginia, because of wages being cut for the second time that year by the Baltimore and Ohio Railroad. By July 21–22, the strike had spread to Maryland, and rioters required federal troops and U.S. Marines being disbursed to simmer the situation. Pittsburgh became the scene of the worst violence with Thomas Alexander Scott at the helm. Militiamen opened fire on rock-throwing strikers, and 300 miles to the east in Philadelphia, a similar scene played out. Scott was president of one of the world's largest corporations, the Pennsylvania Railroad. An estimated 20 were killed in Pittsburgh, and no estimations seem to be done from the Philadelphia episode. He also holds the distinction in some historians' eyes as being the most successful white-collar criminal in American history. Rutherford B. Hayes sent in federal troops to end the strikes. (Historical Society of Dauphin County.)

Thomas Alexander Scott tricked the Pennsylvania legislators into allowing him to create the first holding company, broke laws of corporate involvement in politics, and bought newspapers to sway public perceptions through propaganda. As his corporation moved south, he appointed members of the Ku Klux Klan to the board of directors. About the strikers, he was quoted as saying, "Give them a rifle diet for a few days and see how they like that kind of bread." By the end, 20 were killed and 29 wounded by militiamen for throwing rocks on July 21. Strikers were enraged and forced the militiamen to take refuge in a railroad roundhouse. Strikers set fires that engulfed 39 buildings, 104 locomotives, and 1,245 freight and passenger cars. On July 22, the militia retaliated and shot their way out of the roundhouse, killing 20 more strikers. Rioting continued for more than a month until Rutherford B. Hayes sent federal troops to put an end to the chaos. (IUP Special Collections.)

The strikes of 1877 were pivotal because several key aspects stemmed from them. First, it was clear that John Hartranft sympathized with the strikers, but he was against any type of mob rule or disorder. Also, "one result of this action was the recognition that the militia system was terribly disorganized. As an 'old soldier,' Hartranft saw the need for a modernized body of troops, which led to the formation of today's Pennsylvania National Guard," wrote Dr. Lawrence E. Keener-Farley in his article for the Smithsonian Associates. Finally, after the dust cleared, Hartranft proposed "recognition of labor unions and arbitration of claims." Also in 1877, he ordered martial law on Pittsburgh, Reading and Philadelphia Railroad strikers by unleashing federal troops to assuage the uprising. Defiantly, Hartranft refused to appear before the grand jury to answer charges brought by the Allegheny County district attorney, which also haunts his legacy. (Pennsylvania Historical and Museum Commission.)

ALLAN PINKERTON 1819 - 1884

In 1878, Allan Pinkerton wrote *Strikers, Communists, Tramps and Detectives*, in which he defends strike-breaking to protect the American worker from the union and its communistic trap. With a cynical view of the working-class poor and the "tramps" that the Civil War had bred, Pinkerton's disdain for "whole communities of outcasts" in Pennsylvania, who appear contented despite the deplorable conditions in which they live, is clearly evident. In essence, Pinkerton believed that strike-breaking was preserving free markets, which was good for America. (Left, Historical Society of Dauphin County; below, Ray Washlaski and the Jefferson County Historical Society.)

Over 300 detectives and 200 merchant's police, known as night watchmen, were on Pinkerton's payroll. On July 1, 1884, Pinkerton died. He provided a model that private companies emulated through their C&I forces and set high standards for law enforcement. His sons, William and Robert, ran the company after his death. The boys grew the company to the Pinkerton Agency of today. (Library of Congress.)

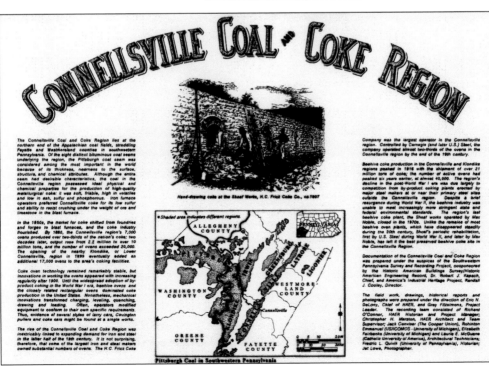

This is an early map of the Connellsville coke region. (Library of Congress.)

On April 2, 1891, the "Morewood Mines Massacre" saw sheriff deputies shoot and kill nine miners during a strike for higher wages in the Connellsville coke region that stretched from Latrobe in Westmoreland County to West Virginia. The mines were owned by the H. C. Frick Company and were a prelude to an all-out war that would take place a year later. Also in that same year on May 1, strikers in Connellsville met the bitter taste of defeat in fighting for an eight-hour workday. The showdown was very similar to various skirmishes throughout the coal regions and the unionization of patch town miners. The magazine on the left is *Harpers* (1897) and the one below is from 1888 and characterizes an angry mob of Polish miners attacking the C&I. (IUP Special Collections.)

The Pinkertons were present during the railroad strikes of 1877 and other labor disputes in Illinois, New York, and Michigan. They garnered the tag of effective strikebreakers, but their true test came in 1892 in Homestead, a borough seven miles east of Pittsburgh along the Monongahela River. "The Pinks," as they were referred to, engaged in a deadly skirmish with the Carnegie Steel Company workers.

For nearly five months leading up to the contract expiration on June 30, 1892, the Amalgamated Association of Iron and Steel Workers (AA), formed in 1876, negotiated with the Carnegie Steel Company to come to terms on a new contract. Tensions bristled previous contract negotiations, but violence did not erupt in Homestead up until 1892.

Andrew Carnegie, portrayed as a union sympathizer, took leave to Scotland as the expiration date loomed. Power was entrusted to his business partner, Henry Clay Frick, who had a reputation for being coarse at best and brutal at worst. Frick was outspoken against the union and wanted it known that he would not talk with union representatives. He wanted direct negotiations with individual workers. With the contract on ice, Frick built a solid board fence around the perimeter of the mill's property, and the barrier was topped with barbed wire. The workers noticed the shift in tone and dubbed the property "Fort Frick." (Left, DEP Bureau of Mining and Reclamation and the Robin Lighty/ Keith Brady Collection.)

Carnegie Steel Works At Homestead PA.

There were early indications that trouble was brewing. First, workers hanged effigies of Frick and superintendent J. A. Potter at the compound and turned away by water those sent to cut them down. Then Frick ceased operations on June 28, and workers were locked out by the time the contract expired two days later. The AA had roughly 750 members, but over 3,000 steelworkers had voted to strike. Workers stalled the strikebreakers, called black sheep or scabs, from entering. Meanwhile, Frick's team of deputy sheriffs and the C&I, who were sworn to guard the property and mandated to post handbills to order workers to stop interfering with plant operations, were overwhelmed, herded onto a boat, and sent out of town by the workers. (Daniel J. Burns.)

Henry Clay Frick saw the difference from this strike to those that came before. This strike was well organized, orchestrated, and purposeful. Hugh O'Donnell offered solid leadership, and this time the strikers were not easily bullied. Frick called the Pinkerton's National Detective Agency in New York for backup, and 300 strikebreakers were sent to protect the company's interests. They were met by strikers and an 11-hour war ensued. (Daniel J. Burns.)

This is a *Harpers* depiction of rioters at Homestead. The battle on the Monongahela River left seven strikers and three Pinkerton agents dead and dozens on both fronts wounded. (Daniel J. Burns.)

The scene was utter chaos with the workers intent on keeping the Pinkertons from landing. Freight cars were set on fire and rolled at the barges, dynamite was tossed, and oil was pumped into the river in an attempt to set it on fire. There was a volley of gunfire that sporadically ensued until the Pinkertons surrendered and were made to walk a gauntlet formed by men, women, and children who allowed them ashore but taunted them, threw rocks and spit on them, and beat some to unconsciousness. Although Frick took responsibility for the event, Andrew Carnegie's involvement or even awareness is unclear. (Daniel J. Burns.)

The workers put up such a fight that the Pinkertons surrendered, but nobody, especially Pinkerton's men, could have guessed that the battle would have raged on as long as it did. Yet the battle seemed to indicate that matters would not be solved or worked out easily. Henry Clay Frick refused to budge, and the destruction that took place on July 6, 1892, appeared to strengthen rather that weaken his resolve. He and Sheriff William H. McCleary dug in and snubbed attempts to negotiate with AA workers immediately after the skirmish, knowing that chaos would lead to the state's intervention. (Daniel J. Burns.)

With the unionists in charge of the plant, Gov. Robert E. Pattison sent 8,000 Pennsylvania State National Guardsmen to the site to restore some semblance of order. It was imperative that the production resume for the company's welfare as well as the country's on a certain level, and it was clear that although the state's guardsmen were to be impartial, they sided with Frick and the company; their actions proved it. The militia took to bullying and intimidating the workers by repeatedly arresting individuals and inundating them with bail bonds while involving them in costly court cases. They also evicted families from their company homes, a tactic later routinely employed by other C&I forces in the era. (Right, Pennsylvania Historical and Museum Commission.; below, Daniel J. Burns.)

Workers mingle outside Henry Clay Frick's administration building. (Daniel J. Burns.)

On July 23, Russian Polish immigrant Alexander Berkman walked into Frick's office and attempted to take his life. Frick was shot twice in the neck. Berkman was arrested and sentenced. Frick reported to work the next day, bruised and bandaged. He spared Berkman's life by saving him from execution. The assassination attempt gained national attention and sympathy for Frick and the antiunion, "anti-socialist" movement. (Daniel J. Burns.)

The strike continued to linger on until November, and although the public thought that the strikers had reasonable requests, the time taken to resolve the issue made both sides seem unreasonable. In the end, the strikers lost their cause, were blacklisted from working in the mills ever again, and some were arrested and charged with murder and other crimes. Some argue that the loss could be marked by the arrival of the state's militia, that the strikers were really crushed by the weight of a state's system, which was in the pocket of big business. The AA was looked at and rendered impotent, so within three years, membership was cut in half. By 1910, it was nonexistent. The Homestead strike was a crushing blow to unionism, especially in the steel industry. (Daniel J. Burns.)

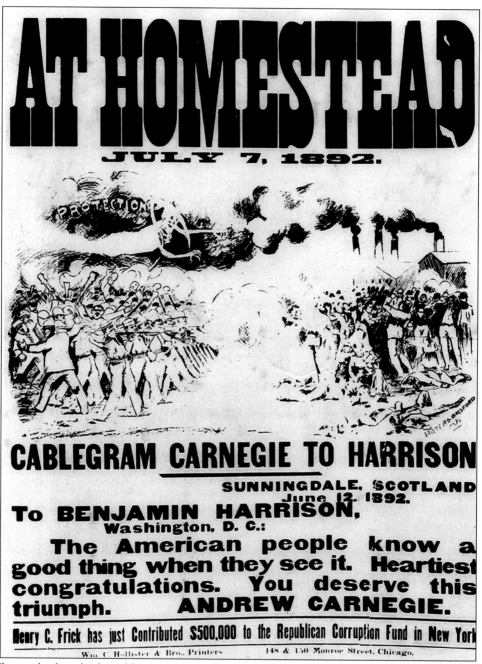

AT HOMESTEAD

JULY 7, 1892.

CABLEGRAM CARNEGIE TO HARRISON

SUNNINGDALE, SCOTLAND
June 12. 1892.

To BENJAMIN HARRISON,
Washington, D. C.:

The American people know a good thing when they see it. Heartiest congratulations. You deserve this triumph. ANDREW CARNEGIE.

Henry C. Frick has just Contributed $500,000 to the Republican Corruption Fund in New York

Wm. C. Hollister & Bro., Printers   148 & 150 Monroe Street, Chicago.

Ultimately, though, the public sympathized with the workers, and unionization continued to grow (again in its grassroots form) in Pennsylvania coalfields as a positive means to combat corporate hostility and injustice. As a result of the ugliness that ensued, the Anti-Pinkerton Act (5 USC 3108) was passed in 1893. The act forbade the government from employing the Pinkertons or any other private police company for hire. The intention was to keep the government neutral in private, corporate affairs. However, these lines blurred time and time again, especially since Henry Clay Frick proved to other company administrators that the state's militia was the key to calming dangerous situations. (Daniel J. Burns.)

Carnegie Steel remained nonunion for the next 40 years. The attempts of the workers proved to be a complete bust, and Frick and Andrew Carnegie continued to groom one of the largest private police forces in the state. Again, it must be noted the impact that the state's militia had on the strike and their collaboration with company police and the local sheriff. Heavy artillery was called in, and guardsmen set up camp and waited out the strikers. They could have waited indefinitely, almost like they did in years to come during the Westmoreland County strike of 1910. (Daniel J. Burns.)

Although workers hated the Pinkertons, their success was undeniable. They were hired to help contain over 70 strikes. The Pinkertons were a precursor to the Federal Bureau of Investigation, whose powers were far reaching. In his book *Broken*, Richard Gid Powers wrote, "The Pinkerton Agency was, in fact, a formidable law enforcement force, with many of the crime-fighting resources and skills that later became trademarks of the FBI, including a terrific public relations machine. . . . All detective agencies acted as strikebreakers, guards, and labor spies, but because the Pinkertons were most famous, they were especially hated as symbols of management violence. Some of the most highly trained, effective, and successful detectives worked for the Pinkerton's Investigative Division, while hardened thugs were part of the Protective Services Division."

Three

STRIKEBREAKING

The C&I's jurisdiction was the entire county, although the focus of control was the limits of the property. The legal jurisdiction was the county listed on the commission form that was sent in and then rubber stamped for authorization. The state took the companies' word that these were men "of good character." The C&I officers were basically guided by their own personal judgment and the whims of the company that paid them.

Gov. John White Geary imposed a $1 fee for each commission, and Samuel Pennypacker wanted to put a one-year term limit on each commission during his governorship, but the employers fought the restriction and proposed a five-year limit instead. Pennypacker compromised and agreed to a three-year limit. Also, during his administration, Pennypacker created the Pennsylvania State Police, the first state law enforcement agency of its kind.

Thorsten Sellin's 1929 authoritative book *Police in America* cited that there was no fee for the companies' commissions for their protection unit. "A list of names was sent to the Governor, who turned them over to a Commission Bureau with an order that so many commissions be sent to such and such company . . . and under the statute their police power was just great on the property as off it." They had no counterpart in any other state. Like small armies that could be dispatched to a patch town quickly in railroad cars, a mine boss and his counterparts could pull together their law enforcement resources to combat any strike anywhere within the state. The goal was to be more organized than the workers. The problem, however, came when company police worked side by side with government authorities and state constables. Although the Anti-Pinkerton Act acknowledged the error in the government contracting private police, laws did not dictate protocol in how the different agencies interacted. (Westmoreland County Historical Society.)

In 1871, a Mexican war veteran with historically memorable social programs, John White Geary, took a closer look at the legitimacy of the C&I's forces. He questioned the ease in which a company could hastily assemble a group of guys, put them on the payroll, deputize them, and send their names in to the state as a binding contract. There was no criterion for the company other than a desire to possess a force and with no fee whatsoever. Geary's requiring a $1 fee created a semblance of accountability and the appearance of regulation with some type of contractual obligation on the companies' part. (Right, Pennsylvania Historical and Museum Commission; below, IUP Special Collections.)

Perhaps John White Geary's worst nightmare occurred in 1897. Luzerne County sheriff James Martin was summoned by the Pardee Company from his Labor Day weekend vacation in Atlantic City to tend to the massive strike that started with the Lehigh and Wilkes-Barre workers' march to organize over an estimated 15,000 strikers from large and small independent coal companies from Luzerne, Carbon, and Schuylkill Counties. By declaring a state of civil disorder, Martin was authorized to deputize 87 men, mostly mid-level company management of Anglo-Saxon, German, and Irish descent, and he armed them with Winchesters and metal-piercing bullets and buckshot. Martin sent word to the 400 strikers that they would be met by company police and other volunteers, making a combined force of over 150 men. He warned them not to come to Lattimer. The striking Polish, Italian, Hungarian, Slovak, and Lithuanian immigrants that made up the strikers were completely unarmed, but they snubbed the sheriff by going to Lattimer anyway. What ensued was a massacre that ignited a firestorm of union support throughout the country. (Luzerne County Historical Society.)

The Pennsylvania Historical and Museum Commission gives an account of the events that touched off the melee that took place on September 10: "At nearly 3:45 in the afternoon the marchers, now numbering over four hundred, approached Lattimer with the American flag in the lead. Martin walked to the head of the column and announced that they must disperse. Not all marchers, particularly those in the back, could hear or see him. Martin attempted to tear the flag from the hands of Steve Jurich. Thwarted, he then grabbed a marcher from the second row. When others came to the marcher's aid, a scuffle broke out while part of the group continued forward. Martin drew his pistol and pulled the trigger, but the weapon did not fire. Then someone yelled 'Fire!' and 'Give two or three shots!' [Several eyewitnesses claimed it was the sheriff, though he would later deny this.] A barrage of shots rang out." (Luzerne County Historical Society.)

As marchers ran and scattered, deputies continued firing and shooting them in their backs. Some 19 were killed and 38 were severely wounded and maimed, and even Sheriff James Martin was sickened by the scene that resulted. News of the massacre spread quickly and made national headlines. Gov. Daniel Hartman Hastings dispatched the Third Brigade of the National Guard to the Hazleton area to maintain law and order, but although there were rumors of a riot, no further significant incident took place. In February 1898, Sheriff Martin and 78 of his deputies were brought to trial and tried for murder at the Luzerne County Court House in Wilkes-Barre. (Left, Pennsylvania Historical and Museum Commission; below, Luzerne County Historical Society.)

Judge Stanley Woodward sat on the bench and maintained order over the 27 days and between 130 to 150 witnesses who testified in front of a continually packed courthouse, and on March 9, the jury returned a verdict of not guilty to applause that was quieted by Woodward, the *New York Times* reported. Not a single "hunkie," as the immigrants of the region were often called, sat on the jury. Workers saw the trial as unfair, and Judge Woodward received death threats through the mail. Some were even released by the judge and made public and printed in newspapers across the country as propaganda to justify the violence against "lawless" immigrant workers. Michael Novak in his work *The Guns of Lattimer* pointed to transcripts where Slovaks were even referred to as "niggers" on the stand. (Luzerne County Historical Society.)

Coal miners recognized their striking power in 1902 when their 160-day strike prompted presidential intervention and the National Guard's assistance, but the strike was a process two years in the making. Headed by John Mitchell, the UMWA achieved success in improving wages and working conditions in the bituminous regions right around the dawn of the 20th century. He had every intention to bring the same negotiations to the anthracite region since wages were stagnated. When operators failed to negotiate with Mitchell, a strike was called, but it was quickly and quietly settled because 1900 was an election year. The William McKinley camp had the means to quash the negative press, and reelection with Theodore (Teddy) Roosevelt on the ticket was fairly easy. However, many of the miners' terms were not met, and so the unresolved issues rankled. On May 12, 1902, being no surprise to anyone, workers walked off their jobs and brought "hard" coal production to a grinding halt. (DEP Bureau of Mining and Reclamation and the Robin Lighty/Keith Brady Collection.)

Over his tenure, McKinley's attitudes toward corporate America shifted from a capitalist, free marketer to a more antitrust, pro-regulation stance, but he did not compare to his successor Teddy Roosevelt, the original "Trust Buster." Taking over after McKinley's assassination in September, Teddy Roosevelt and the nation panicked in October with winter drawing near and a coal shortage because of the strike. On October 3, 1902, Roosevelt intervened with negotiations and invited the UMWA and mine operators to the White House; however, negotiations broke down when coal company officials disagreed with all proposals. Mitchell, as a gesture of goodwill toward Americans, asked the miners to return to work through the winter, but because of the lessons learned in the 1900 strike, workers almost unanimously voted no to Mitchell's request. As a result, Roosevelt took the drastic step of threatening to take possession of the mines and operate them under military force. On October 6, the Pennsylvania National Guard of 9,000 was sent into the eastern region. (DEP Bureau of Mining and Reclamation and the Robin Lighty/ Keith Brady Collection.)

After 163 days, on October 23, 1902, over 150,000 striking miners went back to work, ending the strike with both sides making compromises. Besides the unprecedented presidential influence in labor negotiations, a few aspects make this event significant. The strike brought about Progressive Era labor reforms and a turning point in U.S. policy. Also, a major point of contention was the fact that owners refused to recognize the union as a negotiating force throughout the talks. Another key factor is that this was the first C&I red flag because its actions of brute and blind force and basic barbarianism called attention to the atrocities committed by company police in the course of the strike. It became clear that a formal police force trained and governed with checks and balances should be in place. (DEP Bureau of Mining and Reclamation and the Robin Lighty/Keith Brady Collection.)

Throughout the course of the strike, it is estimated that over 20 miners and mine bosses were killed. Samuel Yellin wrote on the *Militant* Internet newspaper, "By June 2 there were 3,000 Coal and Iron Police and 1,000 secret operatives on duty in the anthracite field. Deadlines were established around the mine properties, and the guards were armed not only with guns, but also with flashlights and cameras to secure pictures of strike leaders for later blacklisting. Employees of the Lehigh Valley Coal Company were notified to vacate company houses unless they returned to work. Accommodations were prepared at the mines for nonunion workers . . . The miners retaliated against the importation of the Coal and Iron Police by organizing a boycott. They abstained from all intercourse not only with scabs and Coal and Iron Police, but also with all persons who continued to serve them. 'Unfair lists' of those who refused to join the strike were posted. Any business place which supplied the wants of those on the 'unfair lists' was deserted by the strikers." (Library of Congress.)

On October 24, 1902, Teddy Roosevelt's intervening commissioners hit the coal fields to investigate the root causes of the strike and areas of needed reform for both sides of the argument. They conducted hearings and put corporate America on trial. Six months later on March 22, 1903, the commission awarded the workers an increase in wages and shorter hours. After an investigation, the commissioners gave recommendations, and at the top of the list was the "discontinuance of the system of employing the 'coal and iron police,' because this force is believed to have an irritating effect, and a resort to the regularly constituted peace authorities in case of necessity." Number two on the list was a "stricter enforcement of laws in the employment of children." All in all, the entire chapter of the 1902 Strike and Commission report was two steps forward and one step back, for John Mitchell and his union were refused recognition as a negotiating organization. Also, although recommendations were made, there was no follow-through to see that any changes of reformation were made. (DEP Bureau of Mining and Reclamation and the Robin Lighty/Keith Brady Collection.)

During his administration, Gov. Samuel Pennypacker put forth child labor legislation, and he took the first steps taken to eradicate the C&I by establishing the Pennsylvania State Police in 1905. By signing Senate Bill 278 on May 2, Pennypacker created the first state police force of its kind that would serve as a model for other states' police throughout the nation. The force was initially divided into four troops: Troop A, Greensburg; Troop B, Wilkes-Barre (later moved to Wyoming); Troop C, Reading; and Troop D, Punxsutawney (pictured). (Right, Don White and the Pennsylvania Historical and Museum Commission.)

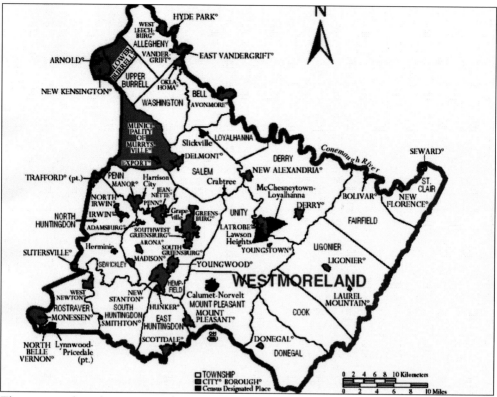

The state police force was a direct result of the commission's report and Gov. Samuel Pennypacker's willingness to follow through on relieving the C&I of its duties. However, there were two problems. There was no legislation to limit C&I police powers, and secondly, the state police was in many terms much more dangerous than company police. This was proven in the Westmoreland Strike of 1910. In this case, the C&I worked almost exclusively as strikebreakers and enforcers inside the workplace during the workers' newly won nine-hour workday, while the state police harassed the workers on the company's behalf the rest of the time. The two forces worked together in evicting mostly a Slovakian workforce from their company homes. (Above, U.S. Census Bureau; below, Westmoreland County Historical Society.)

Evicted men, women, and children were made to spend the winter in tents provided by the UMWA. The strike lasted 16 months, involved 65 mines, and over 22,000 workers envying strikebreakers occupying their homes and jobs. Because of Mitchell and the UMWA, workers had hoped that their struggles would pay off. This photograph of miners living in tents on the Berlin farm is by Export dam. (Westmoreland County Historical Society.)

Stephen H. Norwood in *Strikebreaking and Intimidation: Mercenaries and Masculinity in Twentieth Century-America* said 16 strikers and their wives were killed during the strike, some shot to death in their tent as they lay sleeping. He stated that they bullied their horses into groups of people to knock them around. He contends that this acting out of masculine ideals and shifting attitudes transformed corporate antiunionism and culture. (Westmoreland County Historical Society.)

So many Eastern European immigrants flooded the area that wealthy companies, including the Penn Gas Coal company, went to project housing, where workers were literally corralled by fencing and ushered to work by the C&I. An ocean away from home, they spoke little to no English, so they were easily intimidated, exploited, and in some cases forced to work against their will. The treatment of these scabs was investigated and a hearing was held by the U.S. House of Representatives Committee on Labor. The way they worked in conjunction with the state police and the brutality that both law enforcement agencies displayed brought into question once again the legitimacy and need of private police forces. These pictures came from the area in 1917. (Library of Congress.)

The Westmoreland County sheriff was receiving funds as company security personnel, and he hired deputies to help ease strikebreaking-activity demand. In a 1915 hearing brought about by the U.S. Commission on Industrial Relations, president of the Pennsylvania Federation of Labor James H. Maurer's testimony shocked the commission. He examined duties of each force for large strikes that occurred throughout the region since the Westmoreland Strike and questioned state police duties: "at the time they tried to pass or did pass the constabulary law . . . that they were to take the place of the coal and iron police, and the bill itself . . . creating the department made that provision, or made no such provision; but it did provide what it was to be used for . . . defining their duties, and says they are intended . . . to take the place of the police now appointed at the behest of various corporations. This is part of the act creating the department of State police in 1905, when Samuel W. Pennypacker was governor . . . the law creating the department—the coal and iron department." Maurer is seen on the left. (Library of Congress.)

James H. Maurer's testimony continued, "Take the Westmoreland coal strike as an example of a large strike . . . the deputy sheriffs provide thugs imported there from wherever they can get them, usually from the slums of the great cities, not natives; in very few cases they are natives. These men are clothed with the power and authority of deputies, and are therefore armed, with the right to arrest. Now, the coal and iron police are a little different. He is really more like a detective. He is a gum-shoe man, as it were, in the situation. And word may come to picket men saying that a train is bringing a carload of strike breakers in, to meet at a certain time at the station, and the thugs will gather, and when the train unloads its passengers, these pickets call out to them and say, 'There is a strike on.' 'Don't go out, don't take our jobs.' And sometimes they reach them—sometimes they get in close communication with them and sometimes not. That is when the imported thug comes in." (Westmoreland County Historical Society.)

Maurer's transcribed testimonial on History Matters: The U.S. Survey Course on the Web concluded, "The coal and iron police, most of the time, are on the scene, and when they start something it is because the thugs and the coal and iron police are armed and the strikers are not armed, and are not permitted to be armed; and they are beaten up by the thugs, and that is about the time the constabulary appear on the scene, and they come around, mounted like cavalry, and they come around and see the disturbance, and they always take good care to arrest only the strikers. That is the part they play in that, and when they had this Westmoreland strike, which extended over a very considerable time in Westmoreland County, and not in one instance did we get any aid from the constabulary. We had men who wished to go home, and tried to go home, and the thugs would waylay them and would beat them up, and the constabulary—we telephoned and asked for protection and never got it." (Westmoreland County Historical Society.)

The companies lobbied for advantageous legislation, and the state district court granted them a restraining order, of sorts, that prohibited marches and other such demonstrations that interfered with company operations around company property. They also went so far as to prohibit the use of public roads for such displays; as a result, an exorbitant amount of $50 contempt citations were issued and incidents of shots being fired into crowds were reported. The marchers in the photograph above got off easy; they were dispersed when the C&I turned fire hoses on them. Below, strikers in Latrobe parade down the street. (Above, Westmoreland County Historical Society; below, Library of Congress.)

Over the course of the strike, there were thousands of complaints of severe beatings by wounded miners. Some 16 deaths were related to the strike, all attributed to the state police and the C&I. The state police reportedly shot indiscriminately into the "tent cities," killing or wounding women and children. Sexual assault and rape committed by officers became common claims, and some even accused the law enforcers of promoting prostitution. (The agency never really specified in the claims.) The strike serves as a dark reminder of the terror and the depravity that unrestrained abuse of law enforcement power can impose on its citizens. After the strike and witnessing firsthand the beating of an innocent 70-year-old citizen, James H. Maurer proposed legislation that would abolish the Pennsylvania State Police. The C&I, the county sheriffs, and the state police, and in similar cases the national guard, all coexisted and kept strikers guessing as to who was protecting their rights. (Toby Higbie and IUP Stapleton Library.)

This robust period in the region's coal and iron production history is still looked at today as the area's most eventful era in history. Steel production and coal mining created a boom, and Westmoreland (photographs from Latrobe coke ovens), Fayette, Allegheny, and Indiana Counties rode a wave of financial prosperity, although it was unevenly divvied. (Latrobe Area Historical Society.)

Four

THE RISING ACTION OF LEGISLATIVE PROTECTION

Striking miners made little attempt to disguise their hatred for scabs, the workers who were sent in by the company and protected by their paid police. Straining race relations, one ploy was to hire blacks recruited from the South.

One woman, however, reached out to these scabs and in some cases convinced them to join the union and the strike, never board the train, or refuse to report to work.

The story of Fannie Sellins sheds light on how brutal the C&I could be. Although the plain details of her murder were presented in court, antiunion sentiment kept anyone from being prosecuted for the crime.

A few years after Sellins's death, noted lawyer and ACLU representative Arthur Garfield Hayes was arrested in the small patch town of Vintondale. The incident shed yet another national spotlight on the oppressive ways of the state's C&I.

In 1914, the state launched an investigation of the charges of police brutality against the state police and the private C&I, although charges and complaints had been filed at the governor's office for many different administrations. As the ACLU pointed out in its 1928 report, *The Shame of Pennsylvania*, the only inquiry of any sort was made by the State Federation of Labor at the insistence of its president, James H. Maurer, in 1914. Their findings, under the title of "The American Cossack," were widely distributed. John P. Guyer, a member of Gov. Gifford Pinchot's 1923 commission, published a book of the evidence gathered by the commission under the title of "Pennsylvania's Cossacks." (Left, Daniel J. Burns; below, Luzerne County Historical Society.)

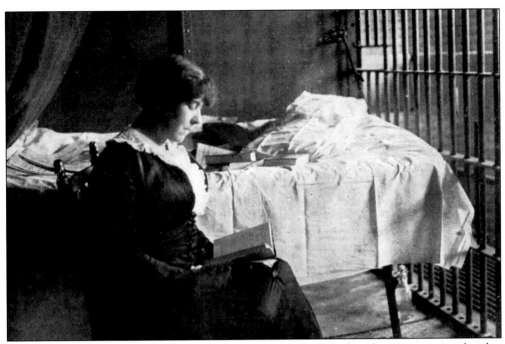

Serving six months in prison for "inciting a riot" while defending her constitutional rights in 1916, Fannie Sellins was given a pardon by Pres. Woodrow Wilson. With a compassionate and steady hand, Sellins's reputation preceded her by the time she moved to New Kensington in the Allegheny-Kiski Valley. Her shocking death on the eve of an organized steelworkers strike on August 29, 1919, illustrated how brutal company authority could be, how corrupt and biased the system was, and how slowly and ineffectively justice and legislation delivers. (National Archives.)

POST CARD

PUT
ONE CENT
STAMP
HERE

Your Excellency:

I herewith respectfully petition you to release Fannie Sellins, at present confined in the Marion County Jail, Fairmont, W. Va., under a six months sentence inflicted by Judge A. G. Dayton.

She is not charged with the violation of any law of the state or nation, but with the alleged violation of Judge Dayton's own injunction, which has been appealed. She is the only woman in a jail containing no provisions for women, and this makes her imprisonment simply torture.

(Signed) ....

(Address) 36

Hon. Woodrow Wilson,

President of the United States,

WASHINGTON, D. C.

Conflicting stories as to the events that took place on that fateful day render the truth indistinguishable from urban legend. Several threads, however, remain consistent throughout. For instance, Fannie Sellins was attacked while going to the aid of Joseph Starzelski who was shot and beaten with clubs by a dozen or so deputies and the C&I. When they turned on her, she ran behind the fences to the left of the deputies in the photograph. She was shot in the back and beaten from behind. She was also shot in the face at close range. The autopsy listed multiple fractures to the head and face and two gunshot wounds. The "Coroner's Jury Verdict" cited the time of death at "4 p.m. due to gun shot wound in left temple from gun in the hands of person or persons unknown to the Jury during an attack on the Sheriffs Deputies on Aug., 26th, 1919." (National Archives.)

The "Coroner's Jury Verdict" signed on September 26, 1919, gives a startling characterization of how the trial that took place in 1923 played out. Written verbatim from a document posted on the University of Pittsburgh Library's Web site, "From the evidence and Post Mortem examination made the jury find death was due to the above cause and the same was Justifiable and in self defense and also recommend that Sheriff Haddock be commended in his prompt and successful action on protecting property and persons in that vicinity and the judgemant excerised in the selection of his deputies. We also Criticise and deplore the action of Alien or Agitators who instill Anarchy and Bolshevism Doctrines in the minds of UnAmericans and uneducated Aliens." An estimated 10,000 marchers joined in the funeral procession, and Sellins was deemed a martyr for dying for their cause. (National Archives.)

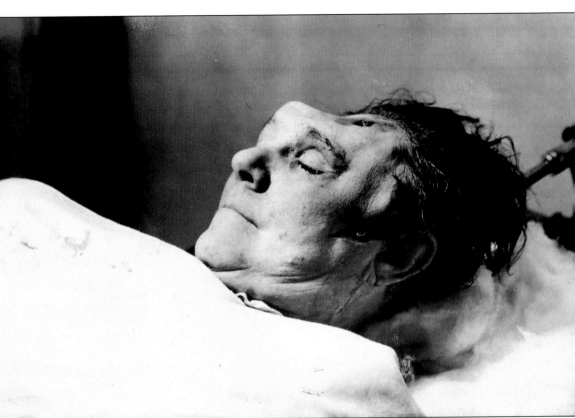

Two men stood trial but were acquitted of Fannie Sellins's murder four years after her death. In a strange turn of events in October 1919, Allegheny County sheriff William S. Haddock sent a letter to the senate committee investigating the steel strike claiming that Sellins's body had been deliberately mutilated after the official autopsy "to discredit those in authority and for the further purpose of furnishing anarchistic, dangerous and revolutionary agitators and organizers propaganda to be used in the steel strike against the State and National Governments, although the incident is not remotely connected with the strike." He charged that the officers were the victims of "a Frame-up." At the request of a relative of Sellins, the body was exhumed and reexamined. The gunshot wound in the back that was omitted from the original examination verdict was confirmed, and labor leaders pointed to these types of tactics being used to defeat workers' morale while striking. (National Archives.)

A letter written on June 7, 1921, from Mother Jones to John Brophy reveals the significance of the little coal towns of District 2. Writing from the Pan American Labor Convention in Mexico City, Jones congratulated Brophy's efforts in educating his district and picking up where former district president William B. Wilson left off. West Virginia was the focus of that year, but the "constabulary" and its "Hessian law" in District 2 demanded attention. Receiving other requests to speak on Labor Day, Jones presented her Labor Day speech at District 2 for several reasons. She liked and respected Brophy and former president Wilson, and she wanted to punctuate her "endorsement" of District 2's work in the national labor movement. (Right, IUP Special Collections; below, Library of Congress.)

Apartado 1855   Mexico City,
June 7, 1921.

Mr. John Brophy,
Clearfield, Pa.
President of the United Mine Workers, District 2.

My dear President Brophy:

I am writing these few lines from a far off land, but nevertheless I am watching the pendulum as it swings in the labor movement--particularly in the Miners organization. I went to extend to you my congratulations for the advance and sane methods you are pursuing in educating the craft you represent. I wish that all other men in your position would take the same interest in educating and developing the men who trust them. I am particularly interested in district 2. It was one of the fighting grounds in the long years gone by when W.B. Wilson was president. You have some mighty good men there. They were always good active boys, they wanted to leave a better condition to their children when they followed them in the pathway of industrial progress.

The battle royal is on between labor and the class who exploit. It will not stop until they come into their own. It has been a long, bitter, struggle, a stormy pathway for the men to travel. There were amongst you some heroic souls--they traveled barefooted, cold and weary to usher in a better system of industrial freedom, but the war is on no doubt between the two forces. The day of machinery and electricity is here and the dawn is breaking into a new civilization. The world is in its birth pains and it is appealing to Labor the world over to come to its relief. Lawyers, preachers, professors, nor politicians cannot grasp this thing. They can't understand what this discontent the world over means, but the man in the tower watching the clouds clash knows before the clap of thunder comes that these forces and elements are warring with each other.

The workers will come into their own, but there must be men at the helm to educate them. They got the material, they make the instruments they apply it to industries, create enormous wealth by it and hand it over the great bulk of that wealth to a group of parasitical vultures. They have bleed men, women, and children. They establish all sorts of hypocritical institutions--Salvations armies, Welfare Workers, Social settlements. Charities Brigades and the blood sucking combination of parisitical lap dogs of the interests live off of the bones of the men, women, and children. They have driven to the grave starving babes, and weeping mothers and broken hearted fathers. The Miners Union has done more for Christianity and for the Nations honor than any other institution in the Nation. They have opened the gate to education. Their organizations have been schools of civilization.

Tell the boys that I am coming for Labor Day to District 2 and I want W.B. Wilson to be there. He's one of the old heroes and warriors in the movement. I know him for many long years and I've never known him yet to fall down when the crucial test came. I have watched him closely and worked side by side with him in the long years gone byand he was always true when the crucial test came. Tell the boys get up a big meeting somewhere for Labor Day and you will accept my endorsement for the magnificent work you are doing. I am watching everyone even at long distance.

I have not been well for the last few months but x I am going to get well for labor day. Accept my sincere regards to you for what you are doing and you can always depend on me to stand with you when you are working for the interests of the children yet to come.

Best wishes to you and my brave boys of District 2 of Pennsylvania. notwithstanding it has a damnable Hessian law in your constabulary. We'll clean it out some day.

Devotedly and truly yours,   Mother Jones

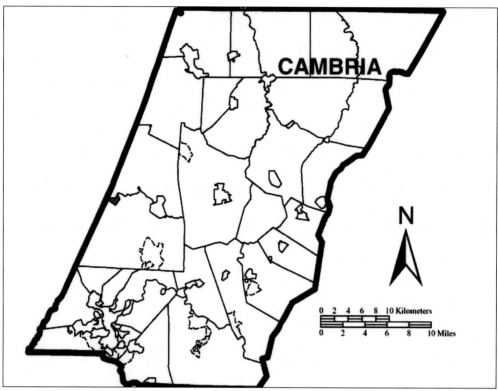

When John L. Lewis called for a strike in 1922, the little patch town of Vintondale became the focus because it was nonunion and nobody entered that town without company authorities authorizing it. With virtually one way in and one way out of the town, like in many others, company guards and night watchmen knew everyone who lived in and visited the town, all the business that residents had and with whom they were meeting in town, and all regular delivery people who needed entrance into the town and to whom they delivered. The atmosphere of the town was one that forced the miners to seek help from the ACLU, which later referred to the town as a "closed town." (Above, U.S. Census Bureau; below, Luzerne County Historical Society.)

Noted New York lawyer Arthur Garfield Hays was sent by the ACLU to Vintondale. He took an entourage of lawyers, union mine officials, and journalists to "break it open" as the ACLU report states. On May 27, as expected, Hays and the group were met, manhandled, and charged with trespassing by Vinton Colliery Company police. Hays told the *New York Times* that was in tow, "They said to us; 'You bust up or we'll bust you up.' We left town to obtain warrants for their arrest and returned with constables from the nearby town of Nanty Glo." Hays returned and five guards were placed under arrest. Although there were great displays of political theater and legal posturing, and although the newspapers made the "armed camp" of Vintondale the topic of good dinner conversation, Hays's challenge of authority met business as usual in the small town that Hays characterized as being "no longer an American city" but a "camp." He summarized, "There is only one rule in Vintondale, the rule of force." (Denise Weber.)

"This terrorizing of citizens on the part of the coal and iron police is no mere incident of the strike," Arthur Garfield Hays said. "The coal companies have exercised complete control over the civil authorities of Vintondale and other mining towns for many years. They employ their own policemen; they close post offices, eject visitors from the towns and hold court in their own offices." One victory for the ACLU was an injunction that an Ebensburg judge granted that kept the company from interfering with union property rights and a scheduled UMWA meeting in mid-June. The National Guard was sent in to maintain order, and Hays's assault case was delayed until the fall term. Vintondale entrepreneurs joined the civil case as plaintiffs, alleging that the company's handling of the strike and the intimidation hurt business. (Denise Weber.)

Denise Weber wrote in *Delano's Domain*, "The Cambria County Court must have ruled in favor of Vinton Colliery in the free speech case because the union presented a petition to the Pennsylvania Supreme Court appealing the Cambria County ruling. The petition was presented in the names of John Brophy (UMWA District 2), James Mark, William Welch, and David Cowan." (IUP Special Collections.)

Weber wrote, "The company guards were eventually found guilty . . . after the strike was over. . . . As for the $30,000 lawsuit against Vinton Colliery, Hays lost the case in New York City. The jury decided he had provoked the assault." The company benefited from the strike of 1922 by using it as an excuse to raise the price of tonnage. (Denise Weber.)

Samuel Pennypacker's compromise to corporations to fix the term of C&I commissions to three years in 1905 was the only legislation concerning the C&I until June 8, 1923, when the fee was raised from $1 to $5 per commission. Gov. Gifford Pinchot's platform in 1922 promised C&I police abolition, or at least reform. John H. Hinshaw noted in his book *Steel and Steelworkers* that a year after taking office, "Pinchot ordered the State Police to review the Coal and Iron Police commissions and revoked 4,000 of them." The form was also altered and more requirements were imposed. For example, the applicant had to be a United States citizen and a resident of Pennsylvania for at least one year immediately preceding his application for a commission. Also, two "reputable references" had to be submitted, along with an "account of his employment for three years prior to his application for commission," as the legislation stated. Republican opposition blocked further reforms. Pinchot's 1926 successor, John Fisher, however, expanded the powers of the C&I. (Pennsylvania Historical and Museum Commission.)

The Delmont mines (in Westmoreland County) also attempted to unionize and strike around the same time in 1922. They also failed because of scab labor and company determination supported by the C&I. Again in 1923, another attempt was made, but it, too, failed. Another attempt to strike and unionize in Vintondale was also dashed in that year by constant surveillance and monitoring of workers' activities. But when the Vinton Colliery Company reduced daily wages by $2.50 in 1924, 600 miners and outside employees walked out. Evictions followed, and the company guards, around 15 to 20, according to Denise Weber, maintained peace. (Denise Weber.)

For various reasons, residents call the 1924 strike of Western Pennsylvania the KKK Strike. But that year also saw the arrest of two C&I officers for beating an agitator, who was arrested for rioting and assault and battery, for attempting to stop strikebreakers from reporting to work. The policemen were charged with assault and battery with intent to kill, a charge that was added by the Nanty Glo justice of the peace after reading the physician's statements. The officers were refused bail and sent to Cambria County jail, but they were never sentenced and were released with fines. Also in that year, legendary C&I Jack Butala, who was known to commonly intimidate residents with his mount, was the defendant in a case of harassment. Backed by union representatives, the plaintiff, who was also involved in the mini-riot and arrested, won her case against Butala. (Denise Weber.)

Public officials were company people in Vintondale, even the superintendent's wife was president of the school board. The same type of situation occurred in Russellton when Republic Iron and Steel, headquartered in Youngstown, Ohio, maintained control of its little sister coal fields by paying for elected public officials at the local, state, and national levels. Author R. S. Sukle writes, "Republic Iron and Steel owned the town of Russellton, located in the coalfields of north Pittsburgh. Russellton, a captive mine, shipped all its coal by rail to the Republic furnaces. During the 1927 Strike, Russellton was the first town to face evictions. Republic paid for an army of State Coal and Iron Police—appointed by the governor but on Republic's payroll—to quickly end the strike. Republic wanted to make an example of Russellton, to break the strike and keep it from spreading from the mines to the mills. Coal an Iron Police seized the striker's household goods to be sold at auction, evicted the families from their homes, and imposed unconstitutional restrictions – beatings, rape, and murder." (Ken Lewetag, www.westdeertownship.com.)

R. S. Sukle continued, "Garden produce stored for winter was destroyed by company agents. Water obtained from nearby creeks, was polluted with mine drainage. No sanitation facilities were available. Transportation in or out of town was controlled by company security guards. The immigrant miners had to stay and endure because there was no other place for them to go. The horrid conditions of the 1927 strike prompted a Federal investigation that resulted in the first draft of the National Industrial Recovery Act. Proposed to Congress in the summer of 1928, it failed. By autumn, the strike had ended. District 5 of UMWA was left in shambles. The Russellton miners went back to work for whatever wages were offered. The last holdouts in the barracks were escorted out of town. Those who still resisted disappeared into the slag dumps. Republic had won." (Ken Lewetag, www.westdeertownship.com.)

Ken Lewetag, a son of a miner, donated the following photographs that he used in his book *West Deer Township (1836–2004): 150 Years of History*. Lewetag writes, "These good-natured, friendly, and loveable gentlemen occasionally made their presence felt in West Deer Township. They were the Coal and Iron Police, an authorized, legal, private police force with a great deal of authority who was generally on the scene in force during a strike. In this area they patrolled the region, which included Harmarville, Indianola, Russellton, and the Ford mines of Bairdford and Curtisville." (Ken Lewetag, www.westdeertownship.com.)

Ken Lewetag captioned, "What appears to be the Seventh Calvary going out to protect a wagon train is simply the Coal and Iron Police crossing the tracks near Curtisville. During the great coal strike of 1927-29, they were a common sight in West Deer Township." (Ken Lewetag, www.westdeertownship.com.)

"The Coal and Iron Police on patrol in a company town. In some other coal mining areas they were called Yellow Dogs, but the name was not used in West Deer. The names used here were usually unprintable." As Sukle and Lewetag both point out, the strike is a part of the town's history that may be less painful forgotten. (Ken Lewetag, www.westdeertownship.com.)

Five

THE FALL

A 1929 pamphlet *The Fight for Civil Liberty* by the ACLU states, "More violations of civil rights occur in Pennsylvania than in all the other states combined. This condition has prevailed for some years. It is due to the industrial control by the great steel and coal companies, to their domination of local and state officials, and to their antiunion policies, buttressed by the most extensive police system in the country. Some hundreds of state police and some thousands of private police commissioned by the state, do their bidding."

By the late 1920s, estimates were 3,000 to 5,000 police employed by coal, iron, and steel operators. In 1928, a United States senate investigative committee was sent to the bituminous fields of Pennsylvania and a 3,400-page report of sworn testimony and evidence from C&I operators, police, miners, union officials, and concerned citizens was the end result. There were stories of beatings, of unwarranted home invasions and automobile searches, and of miners' daughters (aged 14 and 15) being kidnapped and held for days in rented rooms by the C&I. Even though their findings came as a shock to most, nothing really became of the investigation at the federal level.

Also, UMWA numbers dropped from 450,000 to 150,000, and their bargaining power and clout were weakened in Pennsylvania, while they pulled resources and concentrated their efforts where numbers were strong in Illinois.

Because of the egregious reputation of the C&I and the public relations problems they created, 87 companies dropped their police force. Also, in 1929, Gov. John Fisher signed legislation that limited the C&I's jurisdiction to company property; however, after his term, he voiced regret for not abolishing the C&I altogether.

Judge Jonathan Langham, an Indiana County Court of Common Pleas judge, garnered minor attention in 1919 during the strike in the small town of Coral, but this would serve as a prelude to the major controversies that followed. Striking a blow against the union, Langham presided over a court case involving local strike leaders. Irwin Marcus, Eileen Mountjoy Cooper, and Beth O'Leary wrote in their article "The Coal Strike of 1919 in Indiana County and Its Aftermath," "The indictment charged the defendants with interfering with the operations of the company and with those workers who wanted to continue to work. In early July, Judge Jonathan Langham issued a broad injunction which prohibited strikers form engaging in activities which impeded production. By the end of the month the defendants had been convicted of contempt of court and sentenced to jail." (Raymond M. Roberts.)

Calvin Coolidge, who history has dubbed "Silent Cal," took a hands-off, free market approach when it came to dealing with the troubles in Pennsylvania. One of his famous quotes represents his attitude, "Four-fifths of all our troubles would disappear, if we would only sit down and keep still." He saw his lack of interference with company brutality and injustice as protecting the economy. (Library of Congress.)

In 1922, Jonathan Langham raised awareness by issuing a preliminary injunction that forbade striking miners and union officials from interfering with the operations of the Bethlehem Mines Corporation in Heilwood where the superintendent pled the case that production was hampered by "paid agitators." The National Guard was sent in, and along with Langham's injunction, the strike was diffused. The injunction stood strong until 1928. (John Busovicki.)

When similar injunctions were called for in the 1927–1928 Rossiter strike, Jonathan Langham answered the call. His interference and injunctions during this strike gained national attention and criticism. Owning stock in local coal companies, paying some of his reelection campaign with coal company donations, and having a strong ally in Gov. John Fisher, who was an attorney for the Clearfield Bituminous Coal Corporation, Langham's relationship with the coal industry threatened his credibility for critical onlookers. (IUP Special Collections.)

Irwin Marcus, Eileen Mountjoy Cooper, and James P. Dougherty wrote in the article "Judge Jonathan Langham," "His injunction forbade picketing and marching or gathering for meetings or rallies. It prohibited the disbursement of union funds as relief for striking miners . . . newspaper advertisements and other means of communication from being used to aid the cause of the strikers and convincing miners to desert work. However, most of the furor arose from Judge Langham's prohibition against singing hymns and holding church services on lots owned by the Magyar Presbyterian Church. . . . This sweeping injunction and the activities of the coal and iron police helped to give the company the upper hand, but the strikers and the union tried to maintain their morale and to sustain the struggle by holding frequent church services and conducting an outreach campaign." National public outcry and a senate subcommittee descended upon the little town of Rossiter, and Langham's injunction was a focal point. He testified in front of the committee, and he never backed down. There was talk of impeachment, but that faded into obscurity. (U.S. Census Bureau.)

THE SHAME OF PENNSYLVANIA

The story of how Pennsylvania leads the states in police violence and brutality, prosecutions for opinion, and war on strikers and radicals

PUBLISHED BY

THE AMERICAN CIVIL LIBERTIES UNION

100 Fifth Avenue, New York

(1928)

10 Cents

Strong language called for the abolition of C&I forces in the ACLU's 1928 pamphlet *The Shame of Pennsylvania*, yet there also seemed to be a helplessness in its conclusions as well: "The industrial conflict in Pennsylvania will continue to be marked by bloodshed and violence as long as the thousands of public and private police are allowed to abuse their powers without inquiry or punishment. Only a fearless governor has the authority for disciplinary action. Public opinion is apathetic. The legislature can do nothing (except abolish the police, which is not conceivable). Local officials are practically powerless, and in the coal districts most of them are under the domination of the operators anyhow." (Left, IUP Stapleton Library; below, Duquesne University Archives and Special Collections.)

One could pinpoint the exact time and date that the C&I began its decline. It was on Sunday, February 10, 1929, when John Bereski (alias Borkowski and often spelled Barkoski) was pronounced dead at 10:05 a.m. in Sewickley Valley Hospital. Coroner W. J. McGregor's verdict recommended that the three Pittsburgh Coal Company police that beat and kicked Bereski to death from a drunken fight that started at his mother-in-law's house and ended at company barracks with the company doctor present be charged for murder. Those are the facts that seem to remain consistent throughout inconsistent testimony, even though the Hollywood version, *Black Fury*, perhaps altered retellings of the story. Court testimonies made only one thing clear, W. J. Lyster, Harold Watts, and Frank Slapikis unmercifully continued beating Bereski until he was unidentifiable. McGregor wrote, "And as those held are Coal and Iron Police we, the Jury, recommend a complete investigation of the conditions governing the Coal and Iron Police System." One man answered McGregor's requests. (Duquesne University Archives and Special Collections.)

Known from the famous Sacco Vanzetti case (even though his role in the case was minimal) and being a liberal proponent for the underdog, Michael Musmanno (center and left of center in group photograph) came from humble beginnings, having worked as a miner and celebrating his immigrant Italian heritage. He was born from the mold of the "self-made man." Entering into politics, he was seen as a young and overly ambitious man, who was not easily swayed by the system or convinced to conform to the status quo. He wanted to dissolve the C&I but was largely unsuccessful until John Bereski's death ignited much-needed publicity to draw attention to the call for nullification. (Duquesne University Archives and Special Collections.)

The *Charleroi Mail* ran the story "Campaign Opens in Assembly to Wipe Out Coal and Iron Police" on February 13, 1929, the day Bereski was laid to rest. Key details include the following: Musmanno and W. D. Mansfield's (similar) bills were introduced at the opening session; the three C&I officers awaited their murder trials; John Fisher sent Corp. H. C. Johnson of the state police and county detective Frank L. Ritz, the governor's special investigator, to file a full report and launch an investigation into the murder; approached to settle, the widow "spurned the offer," even though the miner and farmer had four children, "a lone ten dollar bill" to his name and $700 of debt. She later was awarded $13,500. (Above, Vicki Molesky and Randi Marodi; below, Duquesne University Archives and Special Collections.)

Michael Musmanno and Sen. William D. Mansfield of Pittsburgh sponsored identical bills written by Attorney General Cyrus Woods to "curb the coal and iron police," wrote Philip Shriver Klein and Ari Hoogenboom in their *A History of Pennsylvania*. "The House strengthened the Musmanno bill to restrict industrial police further. Though Fisher had advocated greater restrictions, he signed the milder Mansfield bill in April 1929 but vetoed the Musnammo bill bringing on a storm of protest. Spurred by this public outcry, Fisher by executive action required that industrial police wear uniforms, that their jurisdiction be restricted to the actual protection of property [one of the important Musnammo bill amendments], and that they be prohibited from 'undue violence in making arrests,' unnecessary use of weapons, and profanity." (Duquesne University Archives and Special Collections.)

On February 9, 1931, *Time* magazine announced Gifford Pinchot's decision. "In accordance with his pre-election pledge, Governor Gifford Pinchot last week announced that when the 1,100 Coal & Iron police commissions expire on June 30 they will not be renewed. 'I recognize,' said he, 'the necessity for police protection in these regions [chiefly the State's western industrial centres], but I believe it should be provided under conditions which will make such outrages as the Barcoski killing forever impossible.' . . . To qualify as an industrial policeman the law stipulates that a man be a citizen of the State, furnish a $2,000 bond, convince the Governor's office that he is of good character. However, the Governor is empowered to withdraw these commissions at any time without necessity of explanation." (Library of Congress.)

The article continues, "Governor Pinchot," an avid outdoorsman concerned about the coal companies' use of labor and natural resources, "proposed a substitute plan for industrial police protection: to have the State pick, train and direct the officers, rent them to the companies in time of disturbance." (Historical Society Dauphin County.)

Time reported, "Civil libertarians pointed out that under this plan all the taxpayers would have to pay for the officers until they were called out by an industrial concern; that persons injured by them would have redress against neither State nor private company, that the establishment of such a system would put the commonwealth in the position of merchandising police protection." Clarence Haney of Bentleyville is pictured. (Pauline and Kathryn Rakosky.)

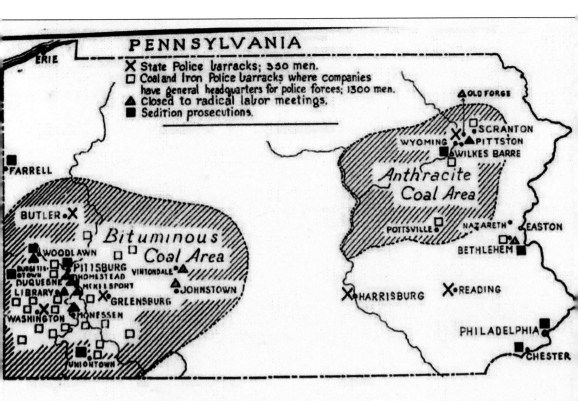

On July 6, 1931, *Time* followed up with a story detailing the death of the C&I. The week before the article ran, two men were killed by deputies, one in a melee at Butler Consolidated's Wildwood mine when 12 others lay wounded, and the other and place in Arnold and involved Pittsburgh Coal Company police. Four strikers were wounded, and six constables and two C&I officers were arrested and charged for murder. Pinchot said, "I have no power over the judges and the injunctions they grant . . . I have no power to prevent evictions . . . I have no power to stop the deputy sheriffs from breaking up picket lines. . . . I am making an honest effort to end this trouble." He also made it known that he would disband the notorious C&I on July 1, as promised. Most of these men, however, would be reemployed by the companies as watchmen. (IUP Special Collections.)

Legislation also affected the constabulary. The elected positions of the state constabulary, because of the C&I, had their duties specifically outlined and their jurisdictions clearly stated. Similar hitches occurred, however, like the known KKK leader who served as a constable in Cambria County. The Pennsylvania State Constabulary today still protects polls and serves the courts when requested. (Don Troxel.)

rner of Lee St across from the
d Portage RR Station

Six

CODA

Although the C&I commission's expiration marked the end of the organized company-paid force in 1931, some mark the official end in 1935 when the stringent Child Labor Law, the National Labor Relations Act, public opinion, and other events and strict legislation reformed coal companies' operations at the federal level, making such an armed industrial force unlawful.

Emergency deputies and constables were documented as being hired randomly and sporadically up until about that time, but no significant event marks their existence. Also, in 1935, Michael Musmanno's movie based loosely on the Bereski case, *Black Fury*, starring Paul Muni and Karen Morely, was released and met with critical and fan popularity. Later Musmanno adapted the work into a novel and published that in 1966.

Also, it should be remembered that the C&I was faced with great challenges. Members were out on the front lines putting their lives in danger, and many were killed in the line of duty. Some were killed mysteriously and then forgotten, like a C&I officer mentioned in an interview. According to a longtime resident, the company officer met his fate on the Bentleyville train tracks during a strike in the mid-1920s. Today no old newspaper exists that accounts the event.

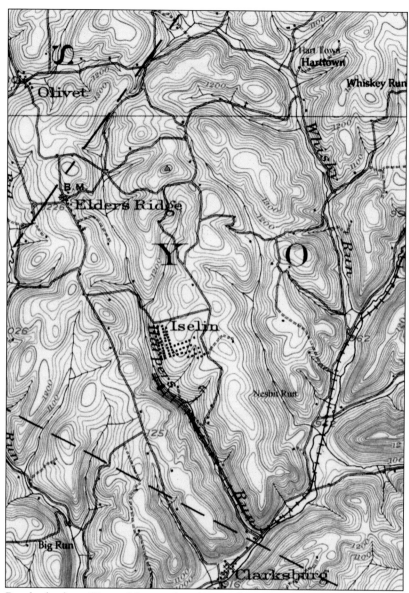

Whiskey Run had a short 50-year life span, but the murder and violence that the town legendarily represents makes it hard for Indiana County residents to forget the Rochester and Pittsburgh Coal and Iron Company patch town. Ever since 1907, when the *Indiana Evening Gazette* ran the headline "Two Men Fall in a Pistol Duel," Whisky Run's reputation grew. From that time to 1926, an estimated 22 unsolved murders took place. Many blame the murders on the Black Hand, a New York mafia syndicate spoken about today in mythological terms. Eileen Mountjoy Cooper wrote of Whisky Run, "While those who can remember may not agree on the exact number of killings or on their causes, all are unanimous in the opinion that, long after other coal towns have been forgotten, Indiana Countians will recall the infamous Whiskey Run . . . where coal dust mixed with murder. Company officials and law enforcement, state police and county detectives could do little to stop the violence or solve the crimes. Similar stories of uncontained, but quiet violence popped up in patch towns all throughout the western Pennsylvania bituminous region." (Ray Washlaski.)

Residents told stories of strangers drifting into town by train. A local would disappear unheard of and their loved ones would be left terrified to talk to local authorities. Other times, as in these cases in the *Indiana Evening Gazette*, the murder victim would be left, perhaps as a gruesome message to others. Adding to the likelihood of an unsolved case was the company's handling of the crime scene and the apparent apathy that resulted from frustration. Cooper states in a newspaper article of November 11, 1978. "Deterred considerably by lack of cooperation from Whiskey Run residents, efforts of officials to solve these crimes tapered off into complete inaction as those who know the particulars of the tragedy refuse to talk, evidently afraid of sharing the fate of the dead men." Constable Harry G. Fulton waits at the West Lebanon train station in this 1910 photograph. Note the handcuffs and pistol. (Mrs. Edison Jamison and Ray Washlaski.)

Indiana Gazette

Aug. 14 1911

VOLUME 7—NO. 291   INDIANA, PA., MONDAY AUGUST

The Evening Gazette Has Become a Necessity in

FIVE KILLED AS RESULT OF SUNDAY FIGHTS IN THIS COUNTY

THE REPUBLI
COMMITTE
THE R

Whiskey Run Quarrel Over a Pretty Italian Girl Ends in the
Death of Four Men—Miner Killed in An Unprovoked
Attack at Jacksonville, the Assailant
Being Fatally Stabbed.

Whiskey Run also a fair share of open-and-shut cases, as well, that were covered by the *Indiana Evening Gazette*. General rowdiness and loose attitudes on gunplay on occasion ended in tragedy, but it was the more sinister Black Hand stories that got the most attention. (Mike Donnelly and Ray Washlaski.)

INDIANA, PENNSYLVANIA, FRIDAY NOVEMBER 4, 1921.

hen Fires Own Brain

'UNCLE DICK' AND THE SCOUTS

Oldest Scout in Town Will Be Host to Local Fellows at His Farm All Day Tomorrow, Says Announcement

WHISKEY RUN BARBER SLAIN IN OWN SHOP

Italian Vendetta Is Believed Responsible for Murder of Charles Lecatta Late Thursday Afternoon.

INVESTIGATIONS

Charles Lecatta, aged 38 years, Italian, and a resident of Whiskey Run for the past three years, was shot and instantly killed in his barber shop in the little mining village Thursday afternoon some time be-

Prospect O Miners H

MISSION FOLKS AT THEIR STATION

Rev. and Mrs. Ralph G. Coonradt Write to Indiana Gazette Telling of Safe Arrival at Tsingtan, China.

The story of Whiskey Run calls into question the C&I's ability to handle and control real crime. Take for example, the two men in the open around a still: Liberty Bertolino and "Joe-Kohn" Bertolino are pictured with a Whiskey Run still around 1925 at the height of Prohibition. (Mr. and Mrs. Mike Bertolino.)

Resistant to change, small mining towns were able to thrive during the boom years, but they were not able to adapt to survive when coal-mining demands dwindled. (IUP Special Collections.)

A case study was conducted by IUP in 1968–1970 in which the death or meager existence of patch towns was documented in a pictorial collection. What part the intimidation of the C&I played in the towns' demise remains unanswered. (IUP Special Collections.)

Towns in western Pennsylvania, like Heilwood, McIntyre, and Black Lick, among others, are stark reminders that flexible economies are necessary for a town's survival, as is a competent police force.

Recent articles suggest that coal, thanks to clean coal technologies, is once again western and southwestern Pennsylvania's future. Towns situated along the Monongahela River in Washington County are hoping for boom years like the past. (California University of Pennsylvania.)

Newell, Pa
9-30-09

Will scenes like this be in the near future in Pennsylvania? (IUP Special Collections.)

Like some have said, companies were able to turn coal mines into gold mines, but many "canaries" died in the process. (IUP Special Collections.)

Finally, the study of the C&I proves William Burroughs correct when he said, "A functioning police state needs no police." (Library of Congress.)

No. 11 Side, Arcadia, Pa.

DISCOVER THOUSANDS OF LOCAL HISTORY BOOKS FEATURING MILLIONS OF VINTAGE IMAGES

Arcadia Publishing, the leading local history publisher in the United States, is committed to making history accessible and meaningful through publishing books that celebrate and preserve the heritage of America's people and places.

Find more books like this at
www.arcadiapublishing.com

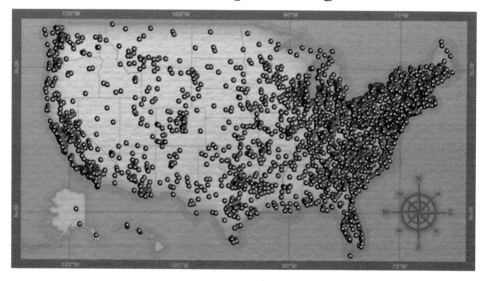

Search for your hometown history, your old stomping grounds, and even your favorite sports team.